Study Guide for Decoding Romeo and Juliet

With Typical Questions and Answers

Steven Smith

Sherwood Press

CONTENTS

— • —

How To Use This Guide

This analysis of Romeo and Juliet intends to offer a study guide to readers who need a more in-depth view of the story.

This book is divided into questions, so the answers appear in a short essay style and may include repeated information. The questions are typical of what a high school student may experience.

I want to think all important questions have been either directly or indirectly answered. However, if you, the reader, feel something is missing, please reach out to me, and I will add it!

Happy studying!
Steven Smith
stevensmithvo@gmail.com

—·—

Why do students study this play

High school students often study Romeo and Juliet for several reasons:

1. Literary significance: As one of William Shakespeare's most famous and enduring works, Romeo and Juliet is a classic example of English literature. Studying the play provides students with an understanding of Shakespeare's language, style, and themes, as well as the cultural and historical context in which it was written.

2. Themes and moral lessons: The play explores universal themes such as love, fate, hatred, and the consequences of impulsive actions. These themes are relevant to students' lives and can promote discussion and reflection on their own experiences and choices. The moral lessons derived from the play can also foster critical thinking and ethical decision-making.

3. Language and poetry: Shakespeare's use of language, including his inventive wordplay, metaphors, and poetic devices, offers an opportunity for students to develop their appreciation for literature and improve their language skills. Analyzing Shakespeare's language and understanding the play's Elizabethan English can also help students develop their critical reading and comprehension abilities.

4. Appreciation for drama and performance: Romeo and Juliet is not only a literary work but also a theatrical masterpiece. Studying

the play can help students appreciate the art of drama and the impact of performance on storytelling. They may also gain a better understanding of the collaborative nature of theater, including the roles of actors, directors, and designers in bringing a script to life.

5. Cultural influence: The story of Romeo and Juliet has had a significant impact on Western culture, inspiring countless adaptations, retellings, and references in literature, music, film, and other art forms. By studying the play, students can gain insight into the lasting influence of Shakespeare's work and its continued relevance to contemporary society.

In summary, high school students study Romeo and Juliet to gain exposure to classic literature, appreciate the beauty and complexity of Shakespeare's language, explore universal themes and moral lessons, develop an understanding of drama and performance, and recognize the play's cultural significance.

—·—

HOW WAS THE PLAY WRITTEN

Romeo and Juliet was written by William Shakespeare, an English playwright and poet, in the late 16th century, around 1594-1596. The play was written during the Elizabethan era, a time when theater was flourishing in England, and Shakespeare was writing for the Lord Chamberlain's Men, a prominent acting company.

Although we don't have specific details about Shakespeare's writing process, we can infer certain aspects based on the historical context and common practices of the time:

1. Sources: Shakespeare often drew inspiration from existing stories and historical events for his plays. In the case of Romeo and Juliet, the primary source is believed to be a narrative poem titled "The Tragical History of Romeus and Juliet" by Arthur Brooke, published in 1562. This poem was itself a translation and adaptation of a story by the Italian writer Matteo Bandello. Shakespeare took this basic narrative and enriched it with his poetic language, character development, and dramatic structure.

2. Writing in blank verse: Romeo and Juliet, like most of Shakespeare's plays, is written primarily in blank verse—unrhymed lines of iambic pentameter. Iambic pentameter consists of five pairs of unstressed and stressed syllables per line, creating a rhythmic pattern that resembles natural speech. This form allowed Shakespeare to create expressive and flexible dialogue, while also elevat-

ing the language with a poetic quality.

3. Use of prose and rhyme: In addition to blank verse, Shakespeare employed prose and rhymed verse in his plays. Prose is used for more casual or comic scenes, while rhymed verse often appears in more formal or romantic situations. In Romeo and Juliet, for example, the sonnet form is used in the lovers' first meeting, highlighting the romantic nature of the scene.

4. Collaboration and revision: Playwriting in the Elizabethan era was often a collaborative process, with input from actors, managers, and fellow playwrights. Shakespeare may have discussed his ideas with colleagues, received feedback, and made revisions as necessary. Additionally, the plays were sometimes altered in performance based on audience reactions and the preferences of the acting company.

5. Stage directions and minimal scenery: Elizabethan plays, including Romeo and Juliet, typically included minimal stage directions, allowing actors and directors to interpret the text and stage the scenes as they saw fit. The focus was primarily on the language and the performances, with simple sets and props that could be easily adapted for different plays.

While the exact details of how Romeo and Juliet was written remain unknown, understanding the context of the Elizabethan theater and Shakespeare's writing practices can provide insight into the creation of this enduring and influential work.

— • —

What are the writing techniques

Shakespeare's Romeo and Juliet is rich with a variety of literary techniques. Here are some examples of these techniques in the play:

1. Simile: A simile is a comparison between two unlike things using "like" or "as." In Act 1, Scene 5, Romeo uses a simile when he first sees Juliet: "O, she doth teach the torches to burn bright! / It seems she hangs upon the cheek of night / Like a rich jewel in an Ethiope's ear" (lines 44-46). Here, Juliet is compared to a jewel in an Ethiopian's ear, emphasizing her beauty and radiance.

2. Metaphor: A metaphor is a direct comparison between two unlike things. In Act 2, Scene 2, Romeo compares Juliet to the sun: "But soft, what light through yonder window breaks? / It is the east, and Juliet is the sun" (lines 2-3). This metaphor highlights Juliet's brightness and warmth in Romeo's life.

3. Foreshadowing: Foreshadowing is a literary device that hints at future events in the story. In Act 1, Scene 4, Romeo foreshadows the tragic outcome of the play when he says, "I fear, too early; for my mind misgives / Some consequence yet hanging in the stars / Shall bitterly begin his fearful date / With this night's revels" (lines 106-109).

4. Personification: Personification is attributing human qualities or actions to non-human entities. In Act 2, Scene 2, Juliet personifies

the night: "Come, gentle night; come, loving, black-browed night; / Give me my Romeo" (lines 21-22). Here, night is given the human qualities of gentleness and love.

5. Irony: Irony is a figure of speech in which the intended meaning is opposite to the literal meaning. In Act 1, Scene 5, when Tybalt recognizes Romeo at the Capulet party, Lord Capulet ironically says, "He bears him like a portly gentleman, / And, to say truth, Verona brags of him / To be a virtuous and well-governed youth" (lines 68-70). The irony lies in the fact that Romeo, a Montague, is being praised by a Capulet.

6. Allusion: An allusion is a reference to another work of literature, person, or event. In Act 1, Scene 4, Mercutio's Queen Mab speech alludes to the mythological figure of Queen Mab, a fairy who is said to control people's dreams.

7. Pun: A pun is a play on words that exploits the multiple meanings or similar sounds of words. In Act 1, Scene 1, Mercutio uses a pun when he says to Romeo, "Nay, gentle Romeo, we must have you dance" (line 30). The word "dance" is used both literally (to dance at the party) and metaphorically (to engage in the fight).

8. Imagery: Imagery is the use of vivid, descriptive language to create mental images for the reader. In Act 2, Scene 2, the balcony scene is filled with rich imagery, such as when Romeo describes Juliet's hand: "See, how she leans her cheek upon her hand! / O, that I were a glove upon that hand, / That I might touch that cheek!" (lines 24-26).

These examples of literary techniques in Romeo and Juliet showcase Shakespeare's mastery of language and storytelling, which contribute to the play's enduring appeal and impact.

— · —

WHAT ARE THE SEVEN LITERARY TECHNIQUES USED

Here are detailed references to the seven literary techniques used in "Romeo and Juliet" with specific examples from the play:

- Iambic Pentameter:
  Example: In Act 1, Scene 1, Benvolio says:
  "Part, fools! Put up your swords; you know not what you do."

Each line of this dialogue contains five iambic feet, with a pattern of unstressed and stressed syllables.

- Blank Verse:
  Example: In Act 2, Scene 2, Romeo speaks in unrhymed iambic pentameter during the famous balcony scene:
  "But, soft! what light through yonder window breaks?
  It is the east, and Juliet is the sun."

- Rhymed Verse:
  Example: In Act 1, Scene 5, Romeo and Juliet share a sonnet (see the explanation for Sonnet below), which is a rhymed verse. Here is the last couplet of their dialogue:
  "Then move not, while my prayer's effect I take.
  Thus from my lips, by yours, my sin is purged."

- Prose:
  Example: In Act 1, Scene 3, the Nurse speaks in prose when

discussing Juliet's age:

"Faith, I can tell her age unto an hour."

This use of prose helps to create a more casual and informal tone in the dialogue of lower-class characters.

- Sonnet:

  Example: In Act 1, Scene 5, Romeo and Juliet share a sonnet when they first meet at the Capulet party. Their dialogue follows the rhyme scheme of a sonnet (ababcdcdefefgg):

  ROMEO (lines 92-95):

  "If I profane with my unworthiest hand

  This holy shrine, the gentle fine is this:

  My lips, two blushing pilgrims, ready stand

  To smooth that rough touch with a tender kiss."

JULIET (lines 96-99): "Good pilgrim, you do wrong your hand too much, Which mannerly devotion shows in this; For saints have hands that pilgrims' hands do touch, And palm to palm is holy palmers' kiss."

- Dramatic Irony:

  Example: In Act 5, Scene 3, Romeo believes Juliet is dead and decides to take his own life. The audience, however, knows that Juliet is not actually dead but has taken a potion to appear so temporarily. This creates dramatic irony, as the audience is aware of the tragic misunderstanding that the characters are not.

- Foreshadowing:

  Example: In Act 1, Scene 5, after meeting Juliet, Romeo says:

  "O dear account! my life is my foe's debt."

This line foreshadows the tragic outcome of the play, hinting that Romeo's life is bound to be intertwined with his enemy's (the Capulet family) and will ultimately lead to their downfall.

WHAT IS THE HISTORICAL BACKGROUND OF WRITING ROMEO AND JULIET

The historical background of writing "Romeo and Juliet" is situated in the Elizabethan era, during the late 16th century. William Shakespeare was an English playwright and poet who composed this tragic play against the backdrop of the social, political, and cultural context of his time. Some of the key aspects of the historical background include:

1. Elizabethan theater: The English Renaissance saw a surge in the popularity of theater, and the construction of playhouses like the Globe Theatre provided a space for the performance of plays. Elizabethan theater was a popular form of entertainment, and audiences consisted of people from various social classes. This era was marked by the works of playwrights like Christopher Marlowe, Ben Jonson, and Shakespeare himself.

2. Patronage and the Lord Chamberlain's Men: During the Elizabethan era, theater companies relied on the support of noble patrons for financial stability. Shakespeare was a member of the Lord Chamberlain's Men, a prominent acting company sponsored by the Lord Chamberlain. This company later became the King's Men under the patronage of King James I.

3. Literary influences: The story of Romeo and Juliet was not an original creation by Shakespeare but was instead adapted from

earlier sources. The most notable influence was Arthur Brooke's poem "The Tragicall History of Romeus and Juliet" (1562), which was itself an English translation of an Italian novella by Matteo Bandello. Additionally, Shakespeare drew inspiration from classical literature, such as Ovid's "Metamorphoses," and other collections of tales like William Painter's "The Palace of Pleasure."

4. Elizabethan language and culture: Shakespeare's writing reflects the rich linguistic tapestry of the Elizabethan era, characterized by the use of metaphor, wordplay, and a wide range of vocabulary. Moreover, the play reflects the societal values and norms of the time, such as the importance of honor, family loyalty, and the role of fate and destiny.

5. Religious and political context: The Elizabethan era was marked by religious tensions between Catholics and Protestants, as well as political rivalries among noble families. These tensions can be seen as a backdrop to the feuding families in "Romeo and Juliet." Additionally, the setting of the play in Verona, Italy, reflects the Elizabethan fascination with Italian culture, which was seen as the cradle of the Renaissance.

In summary, the historical background of writing "Romeo and Juliet" is rooted in the cultural, social, and political landscape of the Elizabethan era. The play was influenced by earlier literary works and reflects the values and concerns of Shakespeare's time.

DESCRIBE THE PLAY

"Romeo and Juliet" is a tragic play written by William Shakespeare that tells the story of two young lovers from feuding families in Verona, Italy. The play explores themes such as love, fate, rivalry, and tragedy. The main characters are Romeo Montague, Juliet Capulet, and their respective families, friends, and confidants. The play is composed of five acts, and each act contains multiple scenes.

Act 1: The play begins with a street brawl between members of the Montague and Capulet households. Prince Escalus, the ruler of Verona, intervenes and declares that any further violence between the two families will result in severe punishment. Meanwhile, Lord Capulet hosts a feast to which Romeo Montague and his friends attend in disguise. Romeo and Juliet meet at the party and fall in love at first sight, unaware that they belong to rival families.

Act 2: Romeo sneaks into the Capulet orchard, and he overhears Juliet declaring her love for him. The two lovers confess their feelings for each other, and despite the danger posed by their families' feud, they decide to marry in secret. With the help of Friar Laurence, who hopes the union will reconcile the feuding families, the couple is secretly wed the following day.

Act 3: Tybalt, Juliet's cousin, seeks revenge for Romeo's uninvited presence at the Capulet feast. He challenges Romeo to a duel, but Romeo refuses to fight, considering Tybalt family after his secret marriage to Juliet. Mercutio, Romeo's friend, takes up the challenge and is killed by Tybalt. Enraged, Romeo kills Tybalt in retaliation, leading to his banishment from

Verona by Prince Escalus. Despite the tragedy, Romeo and Juliet consummate their marriage before Romeo leaves for exile.

Act 4: Desperate to avoid an arranged marriage to Count Paris, Juliet seeks advice from Friar Laurence. He devises a plan to fake her death using a potion that will make her appear dead for 42 hours. The plan is to reunite her with Romeo in secret, and then they can escape together. Juliet drinks the potion and is found seemingly lifeless on her wedding day to Paris.

Act 5: A series of miscommunications result in Romeo not receiving the message about the plan. Believing that Juliet is truly dead, he buys poison and returns to Verona. At Juliet's tomb, Romeo encounters Paris and kills him in a scuffle. Romeo then takes the poison and dies by Juliet's side. Juliet awakens from her potion-induced sleep, finds Romeo dead, and stabs herself with his dagger. The Montagues and Capulets arrive at the tomb and, faced with the tragic consequences of their feud, pledge to end their hostilities.

In summary, "Romeo and Juliet" is a tragic love story about two young lovers from feuding families who are ultimately brought together by fate and misfortune. The play explores the power of love, the destructiveness of rivalry, and the inevitability of fate.

— · —

Brief summary of the five acts

Act 1: A street brawl between the Montague and Capulet families is broken up by Prince Escalus. Romeo Montague attends the Capulet party in disguise, where he meets and falls in love with Juliet Capulet, unaware that they are from rival families.

Act 2: Romeo and Juliet confess their love for each other in the Capulet orchard. They decide to marry in secret, and with the help of Friar Laurence, the couple is wed the next day.

Act 3: Tybalt, Juliet's cousin, challenges Romeo to a duel for attending the Capulet feast. Romeo refuses, but Mercutio, Romeo's friend, takes up the challenge and is killed by Tybalt. In retaliation, Romeo kills Tybalt and is subsequently banished from Verona. Romeo and Juliet consummate their marriage before he leaves for exile.

Act 4: To avoid an arranged marriage to Count Paris, Juliet seeks help from Friar Laurence, who devises a plan to fake her death using a potion. Juliet takes the potion and appears lifeless on her wedding day to Paris.

Act 5: Due to miscommunication, Romeo believes Juliet is truly dead and buys poison to end his life. He returns to Verona, kills Paris at Juliet's tomb, and takes the poison. Juliet awakens, finds Romeo dead, and stabs herself. The Montagues and Capulets, confronted with the tragedy, reconcile and end their feud.

— · —

WHAT ARE THE PLAY'S THEMES

"Romeo and Juliet" explores several themes that contribute to the depth and emotional impact of the play. Some of the major themes include:

1. Love: The central theme of the play is the passionate and all-consuming love between Romeo and Juliet. Their love transcends the bitter feud between their families and ultimately leads to their tragic deaths. The play also explores different types of love, such as romantic love, familial love, and friendship.

2. Fate and Destiny: The idea that fate and destiny govern the lives of the characters is a recurring theme. From the outset, Romeo and Juliet are described as "star-crossed lovers," suggesting that their tragic fate is predetermined. The role of chance and coincidence in the unfolding of events further emphasizes the theme of fate.

3. Conflict and Rivalry: The longstanding feud between the Montague and Capulet families drives the conflict in the play, culminating in the tragic deaths of the young lovers. The rivalry between the families highlights the destructive nature of hate and the consequences of uncontrolled animosity.

4. Youth versus Age: The play contrasts the passionate and impulsive nature of youth with the more restrained and cautious demeanor of the older generation. Romeo and Juliet's youthful passion is set against the backdrop of their families' longstanding grudges,

which the older generation perpetuates.

5. Individual versus Society: Romeo and Juliet's love story showcases the struggle between the desires of the individual and the expectations and constraints of society. The lovers' secret marriage defies social norms and family expectations, but they are ultimately unable to escape the consequences of their actions.

6. Light and Darkness: The play frequently uses imagery of light and darkness to symbolize various aspects of the story. Light often represents love, hope, and goodness, while darkness symbolizes secrecy, danger, and death. Romeo and Juliet's love is often associated with light, while their tragic fate is foreshadowed by images of darkness.

7. The Power of Time: Time plays a significant role in the play, with events unfolding rapidly and often in parallel with the lovers' desperate race against time. The haste with which Romeo and Juliet rush into their relationship and the tragic consequences that follow emphasize the power and inevitability of time.

These themes intertwine throughout the play, contributing to its emotional depth and making "Romeo and Juliet" one of the most enduring and timeless works in literature.

— · —

GIVE DETAILED REFERENCES TO EACH OF THE SEVEN THEMES

Here are detailed references to each of the seven themes in "Romeo and Juliet":

1. Love:

Romantic love is most evident in the relationship between Romeo and Juliet. The famous balcony scene in Act 2, Scene 2, illustrates their deep connection:

JULIET: "My bounty is as boundless as the sea,

My love as deep; the more I give to thee,

The more I have, for both are infinite."

2. Fate and Destiny:

The idea of fate is introduced in the prologue, where the lovers are referred to as "star-cross'd":

"From forth the fatal loins of these two foes,

A pair of star-cross'd lovers take their life."

3. Conflict and Rivalry:

The feud between the Montagues and Capulets is evident from the very beginning of the play, as seen in Act 1, Scene 1, when Sampson and Gregory, servants of the Capulet household, provoke a street fight:

SAMPSON: "Draw, if you be men. Gregory, remember thy

swashing blow."

4. Youth versus Age:

The contrast between the impulsive nature of the young lovers and the more cautious older generation is demonstrated in Act 2, Scene 3, when Friar Laurence cautions Romeo about rushing into marriage:

FRIAR LAURENCE: "Wisely and slow; they stumble that run fast."

5. Individual versus Society:

In Act 2, Scene 2, Romeo expresses his willingness to defy societal expectations and his family name for Juliet's love:

ROMEO: "I have night's cloak to hide me from their sight,

And but thou love me, let them find me here.

My life were better ended by their hate,

Than death prorogued, wanting of thy love."

6. Light and Darkness:

Imagery of light and darkness is used to describe Romeo and Juliet's love in Act 2, Scene 2:

ROMEO: "But soft, what light through yonder window breaks?

It is the east, and Juliet is the sun."

7. The Power of Time:

The rapid progression of events and the power of time is evident in Act 5, Scene 1, when Romeo learns of Juliet's "death" and impulsively decides to end his own life:

ROMEO: "Well, Juliet, I will lie with thee tonight.

Let's see for means. O mischief, thou art swift

To enter in the thoughts of desperate men!"

These references demonstrate how the themes are woven throughout the play, adding depth and complexity to the story of Romeo and Juliet.

— • —

Who are the important characters

The important characters in "Romeo and Juliet" include:

1. Romeo Montague: The young, impulsive protagonist of the play, who falls in love with Juliet and marries her secretly. Romeo is the son of Lord and Lady Montague.

2. Juliet Capulet: The female protagonist, a thirteen-year-old girl from the rival Capulet family. She falls in love with Romeo and defies her family's wishes by marrying him in secret.

3. Friar Laurence: A Franciscan friar who is a confidant to both Romeo and Juliet. He secretly marries the young lovers, hoping their union will end the feud between their families.

4. Nurse: Juliet's nurse and confidante, who has cared for her since birth. She helps facilitate the secret marriage between Romeo and Juliet.

5. Mercutio: Romeo's close friend and a kinsman to Prince Escalus. He is witty, humorous, and loyal. Mercutio is killed by Tybalt during a confrontation, which leads to Romeo killing Tybalt in revenge.

6. Tybalt Capulet: Juliet's hot-headed cousin, known for his aggressive and confrontational nature. He kills Mercutio in a duel and

is later killed by Romeo.

7. Benvolio Montague: Romeo's cousin and friend. Benvolio is a peacemaker, often trying to prevent conflict between the feuding families.

8. Lord Capulet: Juliet's father, the patriarch of the Capulet family. He attempts to force Juliet into an arranged marriage with Count Paris.

9. Lady Capulet: Juliet's mother, who is often distant and cold towards her daughter. She supports her husband's decision to marry Juliet to Paris.

10. Lord Montague: Romeo's father, the patriarch of the Montague family. He is distraught by the feud between his family and the Capulets.

11. Lady Montague: Romeo's mother, who is heartbroken by her son's banishment and eventually dies from grief.

12. Prince Escalus: The ruler of Verona who seeks to maintain order in the city and end the feud between the Montagues and Capulets.

13. Count Paris: A young nobleman who wishes to marry Juliet. He is killed by Romeo when they encounter each other at Juliet's tomb.

These main characters contribute to the development of the plot and embody the various themes present throughout the play.

---.---

IN ORDER OF IMPORTANCE LIST THE CHARACTERS

The importance of characters in "Romeo and Juliet" can be subjective, but here is a possible ranking based on their impact on the plot and central themes:

1. Romeo Montague

2. Juliet Capulet

3. Friar Laurence

4. Nurse

5. Tybalt Capulet

6. Mercutio

7. Lord Capulet

8. Benvolio Montague

9. Lady Capulet

10. Prince Escalus

11. Lord Montague

12. Lady Montague

13. Count Paris

Romeo and Juliet, being the protagonists and central figures of the play, are the most important characters. Friar Laurence and Nurse play crucial roles in facilitating the lovers' secret marriage and devising plans to reunite them. Tybalt and Mercutio are pivotal in escalating the conflict, while Lord and Lady Capulet represent the older generation and societal constraints. Benvolio, Prince Escalus, Lord Montague, Lady Montague, and Count Paris all contribute to the plot, but have comparatively less impact on the play's central themes and events.

Describe Romeo

Romeo Montague is the male protagonist of Shakespeare's "Romeo and Juliet." He is a young, passionate, and impulsive character who falls deeply in love with Juliet Capulet, the daughter of his family's sworn enemy.

Romeo is often depicted as a dreamer, prone to emotional extremes and intense feelings. His character undergoes significant development throughout the play, as he matures and learns the consequences of his actions.

At the beginning of the play, Romeo is depicted as a lovesick youth, infatuated with a girl named Rosaline. However, his emotions quickly shift when he meets Juliet at the Capulet party, and he becomes utterly devoted to her. Romeo's love for Juliet leads him to make several impulsive decisions, such as secretly marrying her and killing her cousin Tybalt in a fit of rage after Tybalt kills his close friend Mercutio.

Romeo's impulsiveness is a defining characteristic and ultimately contributes to the tragic outcome of the play. He fails to think through the consequences of his actions, which often results in chaos and suffering. For example, when Romeo hears the news of Juliet's supposed death, he immediately decides to end his own life without considering other possibilities or seeking further information.

Despite his impulsive nature, Romeo is also a loyal and devoted friend. He deeply cares for those close to him, such as his friends Mercutio and Benvolio, and is willing to risk his life for their sake. His love for Juliet also demonstrates his capacity for deep and selfless affection.

In summary, Romeo is a complex character who embodies the passion and impulsiveness of youth, as well as the transformative power of love. His emotional intensity and devotion to Juliet drive the play's central themes and ultimately lead to the tragic conclusion.

—·—

REFERENCES TO WHY ROMEO IS A COMPLEX CHARACTER

Several instances throughout "Romeo and Juliet" illustrate the complexity of Romeo's character:

1. Emotional Shifts: Romeo's emotions shift quickly, which can be seen in his transition from being infatuated with Rosaline to falling deeply in love with Juliet. In Act 1, Scene 1, Romeo is heartbroken over Rosaline's rejection, but by Act 1, Scene 5, he is captivated by Juliet, stating: "Did my heart love till now? Forswear it, sight! / For I ne'er saw true beauty till this night."

2. Impulsiveness: Romeo's impulsiveness is evident in his hasty decision to marry Juliet. In Act 2, Scene 3, he immediately seeks Friar Laurence's help in arranging the marriage, despite only meeting Juliet the night before: "Then plainly know my heart's dear love is set / On the fair daughter of rich Capulet."

3. Passionate Nature: Romeo's passionate nature is displayed in Act 3, Scene 1, when he avenges Mercutio's death by killing Tybalt: "And fire-eyed fury be my conduct now! / Now, Tybalt, take the 'villain' back again / That late thou gavest me, for Mercutio's soul / Is but a little way above our heads."

4. Self-Reflection: Romeo's complexity is also revealed in moments of self-reflection, such as in Act 3, Scene 3, when he contemplates

the consequences of his actions: "O, I am fortune's fool!"

5. Love's Transformative Power: Romeo's character development shows the transformative power of love. In Act 5, Scene 3, he demonstrates his willingness to die for his love for Juliet: "Here's to my love! O true apothecary! / Thy drugs are quick. Thus with a kiss, I die."

These references showcase Romeo's emotional shifts, impulsiveness, passionate nature, self-reflection, and the transformative power of love, all of which contribute to his complexity as a character.

Describe Juliet

Juliet Capulet is the female protagonist of Shakespeare's "Romeo and Juliet." She is a young, intelligent, and strong-willed character who falls in love with Romeo Montague, a member of her family's rival house.

Juliet is initially portrayed as an obedient and innocent thirteen-year-old girl, but as the play progresses, she demonstrates remarkable maturity and courage in the face of adversity.

Juliet's love for Romeo propels her character development throughout the play. She defies societal norms and her family's expectations by marrying Romeo in secret. This act of defiance is an early indication of her growing independence and strength of character.

In Act 2, Scene 2, during the famous balcony scene, Juliet shows her practical and rational side, despite being deeply in love with Romeo. She worries about the consequences of their love and urges Romeo to be cautious: JULIET: "If they do see thee, they will murder thee."

When faced with the prospect of an arranged marriage to Count Paris, Juliet exhibits her determination and resourcefulness. In Act 4, Scene 1, she seeks Friar Laurence's help to find a way out of the marriage without betraying her love for Romeo: JULIET: "O, bid me leap, rather than marry Paris, / From off the battlements of yonder tower."

Juliet's willingness to take the drastic step of feigning her own death demonstrates her courage and loyalty to Romeo. In Act 4, Scene 3, she overcomes her fears and doubts before taking the sleeping potion provided by Friar Laurence: JULIET: "Romeo, I come! This do I drink to thee."

In the final act, upon discovering Romeo's lifeless body beside her, Juliet displays her strength one last time by choosing to end her own life in order to be with her love: JULIET: "O happy dagger! / This is thy sheath; there rust, and let me die."

In summary, Juliet is a complex character who undergoes significant growth throughout the play. She transforms from a naive and obedient girl into a strong, independent, and resourceful young woman. Her love for Romeo drives her to defy societal expectations and ultimately leads to the tragic conclusion of the play.

—·—

REFERENCES TO WHY JULIET IS A COMPLEX CHARACTE

Several instances throughout "Romeo and Juliet" illustrate the complexity of Juliet's character:

1. Inner Conflict: Juliet's inner conflict between her love for Romeo and her loyalty to her family is evident in Act 2, Scene 2, when she says, "O Romeo, Romeo, wherefore art thou Romeo? / Deny thy father and refuse thy name; / Or, if thou wilt not, be but sworn my love, / And I'll no longer be a Capulet."

2. Independence: Juliet demonstrates independence by defying her parents' wishes and marrying Romeo in secret. In Act 2, Scene 5, she eagerly awaits news from her Nurse about Romeo's intentions: "The clock struck nine when I did send the Nurse; / In half an hour she promised to return."

3. Pragmatism: Juliet shows her pragmatic side when she questions the impulsiveness of Romeo's declarations of love in Act 2, Scene 2: "Dost thou love me? I know thou wilt say 'Ay,' / And I will take thy word; yet if thou swear'st, / Thou mayst prove false."

4. Courage and Resourcefulness: In Act 4, Scene 1, Juliet displays courage and resourcefulness by seeking Friar Laurence's help in avoiding the marriage to Paris: "Tell me not, friar, that thou hear'st of this, / Unless thou tell me how I may prevent it."

5. Emotional Strength: Juliet's emotional strength is evident in Act 4, Scene 3, as she overcomes her fears to take the sleeping potion, demonstrating her commitment to Romeo: "Romeo, Romeo, Romeo! Here's drink—I drink to thee."

6. Devotion: Juliet's devotion to Romeo is clear in the final act, when she chooses to end her own life to be with him. In Act 5, Scene 3, she says, "Yea, noise? Then I'll be brief. O happy dagger! / This is thy sheath; there rust, and let me die."

These references demonstrate Juliet's inner conflict, independence, pragmatism, courage, resourcefulness, emotional strength, and devotion to Romeo, all of which contribute to her complexity as a character.

Describe Friar Laurence

Friar Laurence is a significant character in Shakespeare's "Romeo and Juliet." He is a wise and compassionate Franciscan friar who serves as a confidant and advisor to both Romeo and Juliet.

As an advocate for peace and unity, Friar Laurence plays a crucial role in the development of the play, particularly in the secret marriage of the two protagonists.

Friar Laurence is a voice of reason and wisdom throughout the play. He offers guidance to Romeo and Juliet, helping them navigate the challenges of their forbidden love. In Act 2, Scene 3, he agrees to marry the young lovers, hoping their union will bring an end to the feud between the Montagues and Capulets: "For this alliance may so happy prove / To turn your households' rancor to pure love."

At the same time, Friar Laurence often cautions the young lovers about the potential consequences of their actions. In Act 2, Scene 6, he warns Romeo to love moderately, offering a more tempered view of passion: "These violent delights have violent ends / And in their triumph die, like fire and powder / Which, as they kiss, consume."

When the conflict between the families escalates, Friar Laurence plays a crucial role in attempting to reunite the lovers. He devises a plan for Juliet to feign her death to avoid marrying Paris, hoping that she will eventually reunite with Romeo. In Act 4, Scene 1, he explains his plan to Juliet: "Take thou this vial, being then in bed, / And this distilled liquor drink thou off."

Despite his well-intentioned efforts, Friar Laurence's plans ultimately end in tragedy. He is unable to deliver the message about Juliet's feigned death to Romeo, leading to the misunderstandings and miscommunications that culminate in the lovers' untimely deaths.

In summary, Friar Laurence is a wise and compassionate character who plays a significant role in "Romeo and Juliet." His involvement in the secret marriage and his attempts to reunite the lovers demonstrate his commitment to peace and reconciliation. However, his well-intentioned plans ultimately contribute to the tragic outcome of the play.

— · —

DESCRIBE WHY FRIAR LAURENCE IS AN IMPORTANT CHARACTER

Friar Laurence is an important character in Shakespeare's Romeo and Juliet for several reasons:

1. Role as a confidant: Friar Laurence serves as a trusted confidant for both Romeo and Juliet. As a wise and compassionate figure, he provides guidance and advice to the young lovers, acting as a mediator and counselor.

2. Marriage of Romeo and Juliet: Friar Laurence is the one who marries Romeo and Juliet, believing that their union will help to bring an end to the longstanding feud between the Montagues and Capulets. In this way, he plays a crucial role in advancing the plot and setting the stage for the tragic outcome.

3. Involvement in the plan to reunite the lovers: Friar Laurence devises the plan for Juliet to fake her death in order to escape her arranged marriage to Paris and be with Romeo. This plan ultimately fails due to miscommunication, but it underscores Friar Laurence's active role in trying to help the young lovers achieve happiness together.

4. A symbol of reason and moderation: Friar Laurence represents reason and moderation in a world driven by passion, impulsiveness, and violence. His wisdom and foresight contrast with

the rashness and impulsivity of the other characters, particularly Romeo and Juliet. Despite his good intentions, however, his efforts are ultimately undermined by the very impulsive behavior he tries to temper.

5. Catalyst for the resolution: Although the plan to reunite Romeo and Juliet ends in tragedy, Friar Laurence's confession at the end of the play serves as a catalyst for the resolution between the Montagues and Capulets. His willingness to accept responsibility and explain the truth behind the events that transpired allows the two feuding families to see the devastating consequences of their hatred and decide to reconcile.

Friar Laurence's involvement in the plot, his relationship with the main characters, and his role as a symbol of reason and moderation make him a crucial character in Shakespeare's Romeo and Juliet.

Describe Nurse

The Nurse is a prominent character in Shakespeare's "Romeo and Juliet." She serves as Juliet's confidante, caretaker, and mother figure.

The Nurse is characterized by her humorous, bawdy, and talkative nature, which provides comic relief throughout the play. She is fiercely loyal to Juliet and becomes an essential figure in the secret relationship between Romeo and Juliet.

The Nurse has a close bond with Juliet, having raised her since birth. In Act 1, Scene 3, the Nurse reminisces about Juliet's childhood, revealing her deep affection for her: "When it did taste the wormwood on the nipple / Of my dug and felt it bitter, pretty fool, / To see it tetchy and fall out with the dug!"

When Juliet falls in love with Romeo, the Nurse becomes her trusted confidante and go-between. In Act 2, Scene 4, the Nurse meets with Romeo to discuss his intentions toward Juliet, ensuring that he truly loves her: "If ye should lead her in a fool's paradise, as they say, it were a very gross kind of behavior, as they say."

The Nurse's loyalty to Juliet is also evident in her involvement in the couple's secret marriage. In Act 2, Scene 5, she brings news of the wedding plan to Juliet, showing her dedication to Juliet's happiness: "Then hie you hence to Friar Laurence' cell; / There stays a husband to make you a wife."

However, after Tybalt's death and Romeo's banishment, the Nurse's loyalty appears to waver. In Act 3, Scene 5, she advises Juliet to forget about Romeo and marry Paris, revealing a more pragmatic side to her character: "I think it best you married with the County. / O, he's a lovely gentleman! / Romeo's a dishclout to him."

Despite her seemingly wavering loyalty, the Nurse's primary concern is always Juliet's well-being. Her involvement in Juliet's life and the secret marriage underscores her love and commitment to the young Capulet.

In summary, the Nurse is a complex character who provides comic relief, emotional support, and guidance to Juliet throughout the play. Her loyalty to Juliet, humorous nature, and involvement in the secret marriage make her an essential figure in "Romeo and Juliet."

—·—

DESCRIBE WHY THE NURSE IS A COMPLEX CHARACTER

The Nurse in Shakespeare's Romeo and Juliet is a complex character due to her multifaceted nature, conflicting loyalties, and her role in the development of the plot. Here are some detailed references from the play that contribute to her complexity:

1. Relationship with Juliet: In Act 1, Scene 3, the Nurse's affection for Juliet is evident when she tells Lady Capulet about Juliet's childhood and how she raised her: "For I had then laid wormwood to my dug, / Sitting in the sun under the dovehouse wall" (lines 30-31). The Nurse's memories of raising Juliet demonstrate her close bond with her.

2. Comic relief and bawdy humor: The Nurse's bawdy humor is showcased in Act 2, Scene 5, when she teases Juliet about her marriage to Romeo: "No less! Nay, bigger! Women grow by men" (line 39). This line contains a double entendre, suggesting that women grow in status through marriage and also making a sexual innuendo. This type of humor adds complexity to her character as she provides comic relief in the play.

3. Conflicting loyalties and betrayal: The Nurse initially supports Juliet's secret relationship with Romeo, even going as far as helping the lovers exchange messages and assisting in their secret mar-

riage. However, her loyalty is tested in Act 3, Scene 5, when she advises Juliet to forget about Romeo and marry Paris: "I think it best you married with the County. / O, he's a lovely gentleman! / Romeo's a dishclout to him" (lines 219-221). This change in her stance on Juliet's marriage can be seen as a betrayal and adds a layer of complexity to her character.

4. Ambiguity in motives: The Nurse's motives for supporting Romeo and Juliet's relationship can be ambiguous. In Act 2, Scene 4, when the Nurse meets Romeo to discuss the plans for the secret marriage, she says, "If you be he, sir, I desire some confidence with you" (line 103). This line suggests that the Nurse may be excited by the intrigue and secrecy of the situation, indicating that her motives could be driven by a desire for excitement in her own life.

5. Social status and vulnerability: The Nurse's lower social status as a servant is evident in Act 3, Scene 5, when Lady Capulet dismisses her after she speaks against the arranged marriage to Paris: "Peace, you mumbling fool! / Utter your gravity o'er a gossip's bowl, / For here we need it not" (lines 175-177). This dismissal highlights the Nurse's vulnerable position within the Capulet household and her need to navigate the power dynamics between her loyalty to Juliet and her duty to her employers.

These detailed references from the play demonstrate the various aspects of the Nurse's character that contribute to her complexity, making her an engaging and multifaceted figure in Romeo and Juliet.

Describe Tybalt

Tybalt Capulet is a key character in Shakespeare's "Romeo and Juliet." He is Juliet's cousin and a loyal member of the Capulet family.

Tybalt is characterized by his hot-headedness, aggressive nature, and strong sense of family pride. He is a skilled swordsman and serves as an antagonist in the play, contributing to the ongoing feud between the Montagues and Capulets.

From his introduction in Act 1, Scene 1, Tybalt is portrayed as a confrontational and belligerent character who is quick to engage in violence. His deep hatred for the Montagues is evident when he reacts angrily to Benvolio's attempt to keep the peace: "What, drawn, and talk of peace? I hate the word / As I hate hell, all Montagues, and thee."

Tybalt's hostility is further showcased during the Capulet party in Act 1, Scene 5. Upon recognizing Romeo, a Montague, in their midst, Tybalt is outraged and demands his expulsion. Lord Capulet, however, restrains him, but Tybalt's anger remains unresolved: "I will withdraw, but this intrusion shall / Now seeming sweet convert to bitter gall."

In Act 3, Scene 1, Tybalt's aggression leads to a pivotal and tragic moment in the play. He challenges Romeo to a duel, but Romeo, now secretly married to Juliet, refuses to fight. Tybalt's pride and fury cause him to engage in a sword fight with Mercutio, Romeo's close friend, resulting in Mercutio's death. This event triggers a series of tragic consequences, as Romeo avenges Mercutio's death by killing Tybalt, leading to his own banishment from Verona.

In summary, Tybalt is a hot-headed, aggressive character whose actions significantly contribute to the tragic events in "Romeo and Juliet." His fierce loyalty to the Capulet family and hatred for the Montagues fuel the ongoing feud and ultimately lead to the play's tragic conclusion.

Describe Mercutio

Mercutio is a vital character in Shakespeare's "Romeo and Juliet." He is Romeo's close friend and a relative of Prince Escalus, which places him outside of the feuding Capulet and Montague families.

Mercutio is characterized by his wit, humor, and charisma, making him a source of comic relief and a lively presence in the play. However, his fiery temperament and loyalty to Romeo also lead to his tragic demise.

From his introduction in Act 1, Scene 4, Mercutio's wit and humor are evident. He playfully teases Romeo about his unrequited love for Rosaline and tries to lift his spirits with his lively personality: "You are a lover. Borrow Cupid's wings / And soar with them above a common bound."

Mercutio's most famous speech is his "Queen Mab" monologue in Act 1, Scene 4. The speech showcases his vivid imagination, eloquence, and ability to entertain as he describes a fanciful world inhabited by a fairy queen who controls people's dreams: "O, then I see Queen Mab hath been with you. / She is the fairies' midwife, and she comes / In shape no bigger than an agate stone."

Despite his comedic qualities, Mercutio also has a fiery side, which contributes to the play's tragic events. In Act 3, Scene 1, he becomes embroiled in a heated argument with Tybalt, Juliet's cousin. Mercutio's loyalty to Romeo and his own sense of honor lead him to challenge Tybalt to a duel: "Good King of Cats, nothing but one of your nine lives!"

During the duel, Romeo tries to intervene, but this results in Mercutio's fatal injury at Tybalt's hands. Before dying, Mercutio utters the famous line, "A plague o' both your houses!" which highlights the senselessness of the feud between the Montagues and Capulets. Mercutio's death is a turning point in the play, as it sets the stage for Romeo's revenge and the tragic events that follow.

In summary, Mercutio is a complex character who brings wit, humor, and charisma to "Romeo and Juliet." His loyalty to Romeo and his tragic death serve as catalysts for the play's dramatic events and contribute to the overarching theme of the destructive nature of the feud between the Montagues and Capulets.

—·—

DESCRIBE LORD CAPULET

Lord Capulet is a central character in Shakespeare's "Romeo and Juliet." He is the patriarch of the Capulet family and father to Juliet.

Lord Capulet is a man of authority, wealth, and social standing, but he is also a complex figure whose attitudes and actions change throughout the play. His character is marked by his strong sense of family pride and his often conflicting desires to protect his daughter and maintain his family's honor.

Initially, Lord Capulet appears as a reasonable and somewhat compassionate man. In Act 1, Scene 2, when Count Paris asks for Juliet's hand in marriage, Lord Capulet is reluctant to marry her off too soon and insists that Paris should wait until she is older: "My child is yet a stranger in the world; / She hath not seen the change of fourteen years. / Let two more summers wither in their pride / Ere we may think her ripe to be a bride."

Lord Capulet is also portrayed as a hospitable host during the Capulet party in Act 1, Scene 5. When Tybalt becomes enraged at Romeo's presence, Lord Capulet restrains him and asks him to maintain peace, demonstrating his capacity for level-headedness: "Content thee, gentle coz, let him alone. / He bears him like a portly gentleman, / And, to say truth, Verona brags of him / To be a virtuous and well-governed youth."

However, as the play progresses, Lord Capulet's character takes a darker turn. In Act 3, Scene 5, he becomes furious when Juliet refuses to marry Paris, threatening to disown her and displaying a tyrannical side: "An you be mine, I'll give you to my friend; / An you be not, hang, beg, starve, die in the streets, / For, by my soul, I'll ne'er acknowledge thee."

This change in Lord Capulet's attitude toward his daughter reveals the complexity of his character, as he struggles to balance his love for Juliet with his desire to maintain his family's honor and social standing.

In summary, Lord Capulet is a complex character whose actions and attitudes evolve throughout "Romeo and Juliet." He is a man of authority, wealth, and social standing who displays both compassion and tyranny. His struggle to balance his love for his daughter with his family pride contributes to the tragic events that unfold in the play.

Describe Benvolio Montague

Benvolio Montague is a significant character in Shakespeare's "Romeo and Juliet." He is Romeo's cousin and close friend, as well as a voice of reason and peace within the Montague family.

Benvolio is characterized by his calm and rational demeanor, which often contrasts with the more impulsive and hot-headed actions of other characters in the play.

From the very beginning of the play, Benvolio's peacemaking nature is evident. In Act 1, Scene 1, he tries to break up a fight between the Capulets and Montagues, urging the participants to put their weapons down: "Part, fools! Put up your swords; you know not what you do."

Throughout the play, Benvolio also serves as a confidant and advisor to Romeo. In Act 1, Scene 1, he listens to Romeo's laments about his unrequited love for Rosaline and encourages him to look for other potential love interests: "Be ruled by me, forget to think of her... Examine other beauties."

Benvolio's level-headedness is showcased further in Act 3, Scene 1, when he tries to prevent a confrontation between Mercutio and Tybalt: "I pray thee, good Mercutio, let's retire. / The day is hot, the Capulets abroad, /

And if we meet we shall not 'scape a brawl." Unfortunately, his efforts to keep the peace are unsuccessful, leading to Mercutio's death and Romeo's subsequent revenge on Tybalt.

Benvolio remains a voice of reason throughout the play, providing balanced perspectives and accurate accounts of events. After the fight between Romeo and Tybalt, Benvolio explains to Prince Escalus what happened, emphasizing that Romeo only killed Tybalt to avenge Mercutio's death: "Tybalt, here slain, whom Romeo's hand did slay."

In summary, Benvolio Montague is a calm, rational, and loyal character in "Romeo and Juliet." His peacemaking nature and willingness to support and advise his cousin Romeo make him a crucial figure within the Montague family. Benvolio's character serves as a counterbalance to the more impulsive and hot-headed characters in the play, highlighting the senselessness of the ongoing feud between the Montagues and Capulets.

Describe Lady Capulet

Lady Capulet is an important character in Shakespeare's "Romeo and Juliet." She is the wife of Lord Capulet and the mother of Juliet.

As a member of the Capulet family, Lady Capulet represents the traditional values and expectations of her social class. Her character is marked by a reserved and somewhat distant demeanor, which contrasts with the more nurturing and affectionate relationship Juliet has with the Nurse.

Lady Capulet's formality and emotional distance from her daughter become apparent early in the play. In Act 1, Scene 3, when discussing Juliet's potential marriage to Paris, Lady Capulet reveals that she herself married young and expects Juliet to do the same: "By my count, / I was your mother much upon these years / That you are now a maid." Her reliance on the Nurse to communicate with her daughter further highlights their lack of a close emotional bond.

Despite her reserved nature, Lady Capulet does show some concern for her daughter's well-being. In Act 3, Scene 5, when Juliet is distraught over Romeo's banishment, Lady Capulet initially believes her daughter is grieving for her slain cousin Tybalt: "Evermore weeping for your cousin's death?" However, her sympathy turns to anger when Juliet refuses to marry Paris, aligning her with Lord Capulet's fury.

Lady Capulet's desire for revenge against Romeo is evident in Act 3, Scene 5, when she vows to have him killed for Tybalt's murder: "I'll send to one in Mantua, / Where that same banished runagate doth live, / Shall give him such an unaccustomed dram / That he shall soon keep Tybalt company."

In summary, Lady Capulet is a reserved and somewhat distant character in "Romeo and Juliet." Her emotional detachment from Juliet and adherence to traditional values and social expectations make her an important figure in the play. While she shows some concern for her daughter's well-being, her actions and attitudes often align with those of her husband, Lord Capulet, contributing to the tragic events that unfold.

—•—

Describe Prince Escalus

Prince Escalus is an important character in Shakespeare's "Romeo and Juliet." He is the ruling authority in Verona and a symbol of law and order in the play.

Prince Escalus is characterized by his desire to maintain peace and stability within his city, and his frustration with the ongoing feud between the Montagues and Capulets is a recurring theme throughout the play.

In Act 1, Scene 1, Prince Escalus intervenes when a brawl breaks out between the feuding families, expressing his anger and warning them of severe consequences if they continue to disturb the peace: "If ever you disturb our streets again, / Your lives shall pay the forfeit of the peace."

Prince Escalus also serves as a figure of justice in the play. In Act 3, Scene 1, following the deaths of Mercutio and Tybalt, he is forced to make a difficult decision regarding Romeo's punishment. Although he acknowledges that Romeo's actions were in response to Mercutio's murder, he decides to banish Romeo from Verona: "Immediately we do exile him hence."

His sense of fairness and commitment to justice are further demonstrated in Act 5, Scene 3, when he punishes Friar Laurence and pardons Balthasar and the Nurse after learning the truth about Romeo and Juliet's tragic love story: "We still have known thee for a holy man. / Where's Romeo's man? What can he say in this?"

Prince Escalus's grief over the tragic events culminating in the deaths of Romeo and Juliet leads him to reiterate the consequences of the senseless feud between the two families: "See what a scourge is laid upon your hate, / That heaven finds means to kill your joys with love."

In summary, Prince Escalus is a symbol of law, order, and justice in "Romeo and Juliet." His desire to maintain peace in Verona and his frustration with the ongoing feud between the Montagues and Capulets drive his actions throughout the play. Prince Escalus's character underscores the destructive nature of the feud and its consequences for the entire city.

Describe Lord Montague

Lord Montague is a significant character in Shakespeare's "Romeo and Juliet." He is the patriarch of the Montague family and the father of Romeo.

As a key figure in the play, Lord Montague represents the pride and values of the Montague family. Although he has fewer lines and less stage presence compared to Lord Capulet, Lord Montague's actions and emotions have a notable impact on the play's events.

Lord Montague is primarily depicted as a devoted father who cares for his son's well-being. In Act 1, Scene 1, after the street brawl between the Montagues and Capulets, he expresses concern for Romeo's emotional state, recognizing that something is troubling him: "But to himself so secret and so close, / So far from sounding and discovery, / As is the bud bit with an envious worm."

However, Lord Montague is also a participant in the longstanding feud between the Montagues and Capulets. This rivalry drives much of the conflict in the play and exacerbates the tragic events that unfold. His hostility towards the Capulets is evident in the opening scene, where he is eager to join the fight against them: "Thou villain Capulet! Hold me not, let me go."

Towards the end of the play, Lord Montague's grief over Romeo's death is apparent in Act 5, Scene 3. His sorrow highlights the consequences of the feud between the two families: "Alas, my liege, my wife is dead tonight! / Grief of my son's exile hath stopped her breath."

Ultimately, the tragic deaths of Romeo and Juliet lead Lord Montague to reconcile with Lord Capulet, symbolizing the end of the feud: "O brother Montague, give me thy hand. / This is my daughter's jointure, for no more / Can I demand."

In summary, Lord Montague is a devoted father and a significant figure in "Romeo and Juliet." His participation in the feud between the Montagues and Capulets contributes to the play's tragic events. However, his grief over the loss of his son and willingness to reconcile with the Capulets at the end of the play mark a crucial turning point, emphasizing the play's themes of love, forgiveness, and the destructive nature of senseless conflict.

DESCRIBE LADY MONTAGUE

Lady Montague is a supporting character in Shakespeare's "Romeo and Juliet." She is the wife of Lord Montague and the mother of Romeo.

 Although she has a smaller role in the play compared to her husband, Lady Montague represents the Montague family's values and the maternal aspect of their household.

Lady Montague is primarily portrayed as a loving and concerned mother. In Act 1, Scene 1, after the street brawl between the Montagues and Capulets, she expresses her relief that Romeo was not involved in the fight: "O, where is Romeo? Saw you him today? / Right glad I am he was not at this fray."

Throughout the play, Lady Montague remains largely in the background, overshadowed by her husband and the other characters' more prominent roles. However, her presence and concern for her son's well-being contribute to the overall portrayal of the Montague family and the impact of the feud between the two households.

Tragically, Lady Montague's death is revealed in Act 5, Scene 3, just before the play's resolution. She dies of grief due to Romeo's banishment from Verona, which underlines the devastating consequences of the feud and the choices made by the characters: "Alas, my liege, my wife is dead tonight! / Grief of my son's exile hath stopped her breath."

In summary, Lady Montague is a minor character in "Romeo and Juliet," representing the maternal aspect of the Montague family. Her love for Romeo and her untimely death due to grief emphasize the profound effects of the Montague-Capulet feud on both families, contributing to the play's themes of love, loss, and the consequences of conflict.

DESCRIBE COUNT PARIS

Count Paris is a minor character in Shakespeare's "Romeo and Juliet." He is a young nobleman and a kinsman of Prince Escalus.

Paris is characterized by his respectable social standing, good intentions, and desire to marry Juliet. Although he is not directly involved in the feud between the Montagues and Capulets, his role in the play contributes to the tragic events that unfold.

In Act 1, Scene 2, Paris asks Lord Capulet for Juliet's hand in marriage. Lord Capulet is initially hesitant, suggesting that Paris should wait until Juliet is older: "My child is yet a stranger in the world; / She hath not seen the change of fourteen years. / Let two more summers wither in their pride / Ere we may think her ripe to be a bride." However, he encourages Paris to woo her and invites him to the Capulet's feast.

Paris is depicted as a well-mannered and courteous suitor. In Act 3, Scene 4, after Tybalt's death, Lord Capulet agrees to Paris's proposal and hastily arranges the wedding, believing it will help lift the family's spirits. Paris is unaware of Juliet's secret marriage to Romeo and genuinely believes he is doing the right thing by marrying her.

In Act 4, Scene 1, Paris encounters Juliet at Friar Laurence's cell, where she has gone to seek the friar's help in avoiding the marriage. Paris is kind and caring towards Juliet, although he does not understand her true feelings: "Happily met, my lady and my wife!"

Paris's final appearance in the play occurs in Act 5, Scene 3, at Juliet's tomb. He arrives to mourn her "death" and encounters Romeo, whom he believes to be a vandal attempting to desecrate the tomb. Paris confronts Romeo, leading to a fight in which Paris is killed. With his dying breath, he asks to be laid beside Juliet: "If thou be merciful, / Open the tomb, lay me with Juliet."

In summary, Count Paris is a minor but significant character in "Romeo and Juliet." He represents the societal expectations surrounding marriage and serves as a contrast to the passionate love between Romeo and Juliet. Although well-intentioned and respectful, Paris's role in the play contributes to the tragic events that result from the ongoing feud between the Montagues and Capulets.

WHO ARE MINOR CHARCTERS IN THE PLAY

In addition to the main characters in "Romeo and Juliet," there are several minor characters who contribute to the development of the plot and the overall atmosphere of the play. Some of these minor characters include:

1. Sampson and Gregory: Servants of the Capulet household who provoke a fight with the Montagues in Act 1, Scene 1, highlighting the longstanding feud between the families.

2. Abram: A servant of the Montague household who becomes involved in the street brawl in Act 1, Scene 1.

3. Peter: A servant of the Capulet household who is often portrayed as comical. He appears in several scenes, including the one where he invites guests to the Capulet party.

4. Friar John: A Franciscan friar who is entrusted with the task of delivering Friar Laurence's letter to Romeo about Juliet's feigned death. His failure to deliver the letter results in the tragic misunderstanding that leads to the deaths of Romeo and Juliet.

5. Balthasar: Romeo's personal servant, who brings him the news of Juliet's "death" in Act 5, inadvertently setting the tragic conclusion of the play in motion.

6. Apothecary: A poor pharmacist in Mantua who illegally sells

poison to Romeo. The Apothecary's desperation for money and Romeo's desperation for a means to end his life highlight the darker aspects of the play.

7. The First and Second Watchmen: The guards who discover the bodies of Paris, Romeo, and Juliet in the Capulet tomb, and who summon the other characters to the scene.

8. The Musicians: A group of musicians who provide comic relief in the play, appearing in Act 4, Scene 5, after the discovery of Juliet's "lifeless" body.

These minor characters may not play central roles in the development of the main themes, but they contribute to the overall structure and progression of the plot, as well as to the atmosphere and tone of the play.

— · —

WHAT IS THE SYMBOLISM IN THE PLAY

There is symbolism throughout Shakespeare's Romeo and Juliet, with certain symbols helping to reinforce the play's themes and emotions. Some notable examples include:

1. Light and Darkness: The recurring imagery of light and darkness is used to symbolize the contrast between love and hate, as well as the ephemeral nature of happiness. Romeo often refers to Juliet as a source of light, such as in Act 2, Scene 2, when he says, "But soft, what light through yonder window breaks? / It is the east, and Juliet is the sun" (lines 2-3). The contrast between light and darkness symbolizes the stark difference between the lovers' passionate love and the violent hatred of their feuding families.

2. Poison: Poison is a symbol of the destructive power of both love and hate. The poison Romeo uses to end his life in Act 5, Scene 3, represents the tragic outcome of their love, which has been tainted by the hatred between their families. The poison also serves as a metaphor for the corrosive nature of the Montagues' and Capulets' enmity.

3. The Queen Mab speech: In Act 1, Scene 4, Mercutio delivers the famous Queen Mab speech, describing a mischievous fairy who brings dreams to humans. Queen Mab can be seen as a symbol of the unpredictable nature of dreams, desires, and passions. Her

influence over people's dreams suggests that human desires can be both whimsical and powerful, leading to unintended consequences.

4. The Balcony: The balcony scene in Act 2, Scene 2, is one of the most iconic moments in the play. The physical separation between Romeo and Juliet on the balcony symbolizes the barriers and obstacles they face as a result of their feuding families. Despite their love, the distance between them foreshadows the tragic events to come.

5. The Dagger: The dagger that Juliet uses to end her life in Act 5, Scene 3, symbolizes the violent consequences of the lovers' forbidden love, as well as the power of fate. Juliet's use of the dagger also demonstrates her desperation and determination to be with Romeo, even in death.

These symbols in Romeo and Juliet help to convey the play's central themes and emotions, enriching the audience's understanding of the story and its characters.

— · —

DETAILED REFERENCES TO EACH CONFLICT

Here are the detailed references to each conflict in "Romeo and Juliet":

1. Feud between the Montagues and Capulets: The feud between the Montagues and Capulets is introduced in the opening scene of the play when a street brawl breaks out between the two families. The ongoing conflict between the two households is characterized by violence, hatred, and a refusal to compromise. The feud drives much of the play's conflict and exacerbates the tragic events that unfold. Examples of this conflict can be seen throughout the play, including in Act 1, Scene 1, when Prince Escalus warns the families of severe consequences if they continue to disturb the peace. In Act 3, Scene 1, Tybalt kills Mercutio, Romeo kills Tybalt, and the feud escalates, leading to Romeo's banishment and the tragic events that follow.

2. Romeo's internal conflict: Romeo is conflicted between his love for Juliet and his loyalty to his family and their feud with the Capulets. This conflict is first introduced in Act 1, Scene 1, when Romeo expresses his frustration with love and his sorrow over Rosaline's rejection: "Out of her favor where I am in love." In Act 2, Scene 2, Romeo declares his love for Juliet and expresses his internal conflict: "My name, dear saint, is hateful to myself, / Because it is an enemy to thee." Romeo's internal conflict drives

his actions throughout the play, leading to his secret marriage to Juliet and his eventual tragic end.

3. Romeo and Juliet's forbidden love: The central conflict of the play is the forbidden love between Romeo and Juliet. Their love is opposed by their families and the societal expectations surrounding marriage. Examples of this conflict can be seen throughout the play, including in Act 2, Scene 2, when Romeo and Juliet declare their love for each other and acknowledge the obstacles they face: "What's in a name? That which we call a rose / By any other name would smell as sweet." The conflict between their families and societal expectations lead to secrecy, deception, and ultimately tragedy.

4. Tybalt's aggression: Tybalt's aggressive nature and his hatred for the Montagues fuel the conflict between the two families. This conflict is first introduced in Act 1, Scene 1, when Tybalt expresses his hatred for the Montagues and tries to start a fight: "What, drawn and talk of peace? I hate the word / As I hate hell, all Montagues, and thee." Tybalt's aggression leads to several violent confrontations throughout the play, including the deaths of Mercutio and Tybalt.

5. Parental authority and rebellion: The conflict between parental authority and rebellion is evident in the relationship between Juliet and her parents, who try to force her into a marriage with Paris. Examples of this conflict can be seen in Act 3, Scene 5, when Juliet defies her parents' wishes and refuses to marry Paris: "Now by Saint Peter's Church and Peter too, / He shall not make me there a joyful bride." Juliet's rebellion against her parents' authority leads to secrecy, deception, and ultimately tragedy.

—— • ——

WHAT IS THE CLIMAX OF THE PLAY

The climax of Shakespeare's Romeo and Juliet occurs in Act 3, Scene 1, when Mercutio and Tybalt are killed in a street brawl, and Romeo is subsequently banished from Verona. This pivotal scene marks the turning point of the play, as the tragic consequences of the characters' actions begin to unfold.

1. Tybalt's challenge: The scene begins with Tybalt challenging Romeo to a duel as a result of Romeo's uninvited appearance at the Capulet's masquerade ball. However, Romeo refuses to fight Tybalt, as he is now secretly married to Juliet and considers Tybalt family: "I do protest, I never injured thee / But love thee better than thou canst devise" (lines 66-67).

2. Mercutio's intervention: Mercutio, angered by Romeo's refusal to fight and Tybalt's taunts, steps in and takes up the challenge himself. As Romeo tries to intervene and stop the fight, Tybalt inadvertently stabs Mercutio under Romeo's arm: "I am hurt. / A plague o' both your houses! I am sped" (lines 90-91). Mercutio's death marks the beginning of the tragic turn in the play.

3. Romeo's revenge: Overcome with guilt and anger, Romeo avenges Mercutio's death by engaging in a fight with Tybalt and ultimately killing him: "And fire-eyed fury be my conduct now! / Now, Tybalt, take the 'villain' back again / That late thou gavest

me" (lines 123-125).

4. Romeo's banishment: After Tybalt's death, the Prince of Verona, who had previously warned the Montagues and Capulets that further bloodshed would result in severe punishment, banishes Romeo from Verona: "And for that offence / Immediately we do exile him hence" (lines 186-187). This banishment sets in motion the series of miscommunications and tragic events that ultimately lead to Romeo and Juliet's deaths.

The climax in Act 3, Scene 1 brings together the play's central themes of love, hatred, and the consequences of impulsive actions. It serves as a turning point where the tragic fates of the main characters become inevitable, and the hope for a peaceful resolution between the feuding families begins to fade.

—·—

WHAT IS THE MORAL OF THE STORY

The moral of the story of Shakespeare's Romeo and Juliet is open to interpretation, as different people may take away different lessons from the play. However, some common themes and morals include:

1. The dangers of hasty and impulsive actions: Romeo and Juliet's rash decisions and impulsive behavior ultimately lead to their tragic end. Their inability to slow down, think rationally, and consider the consequences of their actions plays a significant role in their fate.

2. The destructiveness of feuds and hatred: The ongoing feud between the Montagues and Capulets is a central element of the play. This senseless hatred not only perpetuates violence and suffering but also contributes to the tragic outcome of the play. The moral here is that hatred and enmity can cause immense pain and destruction, and reconciliation is crucial for a peaceful society.

3. The power of love and its potential for both good and bad: Love is a powerful force that can bring people together but can also lead to their downfall. While Romeo and Juliet's love for each other helps to humanize the characters and highlight the value of love, their intense passion and inability to see beyond their immediate desires contribute to their tragic end. Thus, the play serves as a cautionary tale about the potential consequences of unchecked

love and passion.

4. The role of fate and free will: Shakespeare explores the themes of fate and free will throughout the play, leaving the audience to ponder the extent to which the characters' actions and the outcome of the play are predestined or a result of their choices. This can serve as a reminder that while we may not have control over every aspect of our lives, we still have the power to make choices and shape our destiny.

5. Communication and understanding: A lack of clear communication and understanding between characters contributes to the tragic outcome of Romeo and Juliet. This emphasizes the importance of open and honest communication, as well as the need for empathy and understanding in relationships.

www.ingramcontent.com/pod-product-compliance
Lightning Source LLC
Chambersburg PA
CBHW031253120626

46545CB00007B/2796